child of the moon

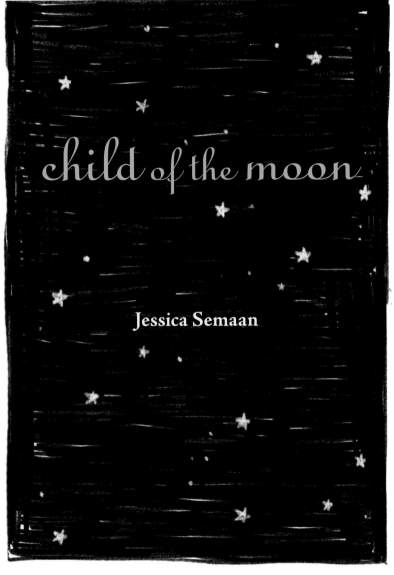

child of the moon

Jessica Semaan

Andrews McMeel
PUBLISHING®

child of the moon

Andrews McMeel Publishing
a division of Andrews McMeel Universal
1130 Walnut Street, Kansas City, Missouri 64106

www.andrewsmcmeel.com

19 20 21 22 23 TEN 10 9 8 7 6 5 4 3 2 1

ISBN: 978-1-4494-9448-3

Library of Congress Control Number: 2018951477

Illustrator: Nour I. Flayhan
Editor: Allison Adler
Art Director/Designer: Diane Marsh
Production Editor: Margaret Utz
Production Manager: Tamara Haus

ATTENTION: SCHOOLS AND BUSINESSES
Andrews McMeel books are available at quantity discounts with bulk purchase for educational, business, or sales promotional use. For information, please e-mail the Andrews McMeel Publishing Special Sales Department: specialsales@amuniversal.com.

To my mother and grandmothers

contents

introduction   ix

Blood Moon   1

Half Moon   25

New Moon   59

Flower Moon   135

acknowledgments   179
about the author   181

introduction

I packed an empty notebook, my comfy pants, and Pema Chödrön's *When Things Fall Apart*, and I drove very far. Carrying the baggage of *fear*, *shame*, and *despair*, I took refuge at a writing retreat in the mountains of Santa Cruz. I traveled far to write this book, began it while battling with *fear*, *shame*, and *despair*, with no glimpse of hope.

For a long time, I have been on the hunt for their origins. I wanted to know *why* they had chosen me as their friend in sin.

I screamed *why* in every forest of California. I yelled *why* in every desert of Arabia.

Nothing. I got silence, and as I write this, I still have silence.

Bathing in tears of silence, I finally noticed the moon, who has always been there to soothe. Especially on the darkest nights of the year. For even a waning or waxing crescent moon, as thin as it is, is still there. The moon was the love that made the questions of *why* my life was like this, and *why* my pain was so overwhelming, wither away like autumn leaves.

Sailing in the sea of silence, I heard echoes of my *whys*. Other voices were screaming desperate whys. *Whys* from every language, every continent, every ethnicity, every age, every place. I was screaming *why* with you, you who were hurting, too.

Sinking into the hole of silence, I heard her sobs. The child said: *"Love me please."* She seemed indifferent to my *whys*. She seemed unfazed by the silence. She seemed unconcerned with my adult drama. She wanted love from her mama.

I write this book for her, the **child of the moon**. She is standing at the abyss of the unknown in the light of a full moon. She is ready to jump, but the fear is pulling her back.

I write this book for you, all **children of the moon**. Those of you who feel unloved, misunderstood, unseen. Those of you who are relentlessly seeking to know *why*, *why* you. *Why* fear, shame, and despair chose you.

I write this book for you, **children of the moon**, to remind you that there is always the moon. In all its phases, and stages, and shapes, and meanings. The moon sees you even on the nights you can't see through.

I visited the darkness
and returned with a
book of poetry

When I dance, I dance with you
When I sing, I sing for you
When I write, I write to you
When I breathe, I breathe through you
To the women that sweat, cried, bled for me
I dedicate this ink to you

You are a child of the moon if

They bullied you

They invaded your body and stole your safety

They neglected you, your emotions, and your needs

They oppressed your talents, your voice, your sexuality, your freedom

They abused you verbally

They abused you physically

They were not there when you needed them to protect you

They denied your emotions, no matter how big or small they were

They ignored your triumphs and little wins

They punished you for being vulnerable

They reminded you of your mistakes and shamed you for them

They stole or destroyed your home

Dreams, while writing this book

*Sitting in a room with hundreds of people, trying to give them the
    book, they each refuse*
No one will read it

*Mother transcribing my book in a journal yelling, crying, and
    damning me*
What will my family say?

Trying to write, my fingers melting
What if I can't write it?

In between being your mother and father, I forgot to be your
  daughter
And became the child of the moon

You and I
In shame in pain
Sister,
I promise
It won't be in vain

blood moon

Beirut, 1988

The question of why me has haunted me

You put a machine gun to my head, you got her on her knees

Decades later, an unanswered question and a traumatized
    brain

This terror is hard to shake

I tried meditation and it has been the same

For all this time I thought I was insane

That was the only way to explain the pain

Then I educated myself

I wanted to solve this for the both of us

Because I deserve to be loved

Because you deserve to be loved

Confusion

How can he love me and touch me?

Confusion

How can it feel good and be so wrong?

Confusion

How can she love me and hit me?

Confusion

How can they be adults, and act like children?

Confusion

You were supposed to be the sun and the moon and I the star
Feeding on your light, basking in your shadow

You were supposed to be the water and the soil and I the flower
Flourishing from within you into the world

You were supposed to be the rudder and the sail and I the ship
Guiding me into a safe shore

You were supposed to be the mother and the father and I the
child
Feeding on your milk, sleeping in your arms

Instead you were two children fighting and drowning and
dragging me down with you

The bystander
You gave me love, affection
You were the only one I trusted
Yet you stood there witnessing the beating
Saying nothing
How can I reconcile your silence and your love?

The mourning

I searched for your love in the wrong places
The healing arms of shamans
The loud prayers of ashrams
The stillness of Buddhist monasteries
The softness of protective fairies
The soothing words of other mothers
The bottomless edge when I suffer
I roamed, starved, begged
And when I gave up
I saw the mourning
And I wept

Suicidal fantasy
She will finally hold me close
There, dead in her arms
Regretting all the harm
She will see
A beauty mark on my left cheek
Imperfections and wisps of curls
Then she will come to love me
Like a mother loves a daughter
Bathing my body in the freshest rose water

The loaf of bread
I waited, nose smashed against the window
Counting the bombs, praying they did not hit you
You said we needed a loaf of bread
But you did not return at sunset
I imagined you dead

The pain that never goes away
When the person you love the most
Leaves you when you need them the most

To have a narcissistic parent
Is to believe the whole universe's calamities are your making
Because they blamed it on you
To have a narcissistic parent
Is to believe you have to constantly prove that you are worthy
of love
Because their version of love is conditional and fleeting
To have a narcissistic parent
Is to seek approval from anyone and everyone
Because as a child you begged and prayed for one smile that
rarely came
To have a narcissistic parent
Is to deny your mistakes, weaknesses, and vulnerabilities
Because you are a projection of them, and they are never
wrong, never weak, never in need
To have a narcissistic parent
Is to become an expert at manipulation, not out of choice
Because you saw them charm the whole universe, the same
universe who never understood your suffering
To have a narcissistic parent
Is to become the parent of your parent
Because all you see is a child throwing tantrums, so you adult
up
To have a narcissistic parent
Is to struggle in love
Because you assume they will all leave you just like they did
To have a narcissistic parent
Is to choose the healer, caregiver, artist path

Because you know loss and darkness too well

Because perhaps deep down inside, you would hope to one day
    save them

To have a narcissistic parent

Is heart wrenching because you see them destroy themselves

Because their trauma must have been so painful, letting down
    the wall will burn them alive

In between feeling angry, unheard, unseen, and in a constant
    search for the love you never received

You start seeing these moments of acceptance, you surprise
    yourself by putting up boundaries, you give yourself approval
    just because

And slowly you realize that you have all the love in you

And you begin seeing them for who they really are

A terrified child seeking love, just like you

Perfectionism

I could have turned out an alcoholic or a drug addict. Instead I was addicted to my mother's bread crumbs of acceptance

the sound of the militia
machine guns was a breeze
compared to their verbal storms

A tragedy
My parents are dead
And alive

Shelter distractions
A moon gate
Rose out from the rubble
Behind it lay the gardens of Isfahan

The sound of the Israeli jets
Crouching on the balcony, dripping in sweat
Alone in my plight
I took refuge in the moon so bright

Childhood trauma #1

The body is the most dangerous place to be

Childhood trauma #2

When the feelings of terror are too much for your little body

When the events are too much to process for your fresh
growing brain

Your life from there on is fighting, freezing, fleeing, to survive
what was not yours all along

Childhood trauma #3

My body is one of a four-year-old hostage

My brain is one of a forty-year-old lizard

Childhood trauma #4
Danger is safe
Joy is dangerous

Childhood trauma #5

My mind can't comprehend what it would be like to have my needs met

Despair

Despair is calling her name
Despair knows the game
Despair feels like home
Despair won't leave her alone

She is fragile like a dead flower
Her petals fall by the hour
She is three or four
She sees no sky to soar

I am struggling to look at her again
She reminds me of rotten pain
Buried in rubble of shame
Smelling like gunpowder and flames

She is looking for me
She is ready to be free
Am I ready to be free?

I know tomorrow will come with another excuse
Of why I could not save her from the abuse
But tomorrow I stay
For despair no longer scares me away
I know its ins and outs
I know how it laughs and how it cries
I know better not to believe the stories
I might be ready to give her back a life of glory

half moon

Lisbon, 2016

I woke up in sweats. It took me a couple of minutes to orient. I was in Lisbon. In a hostel. I was safe. I could not go back to sleep. I wrote my therapist:

The memories of the abuse are flashing in my dreams. I think I am ready.

I had to stop my life. My work. My routine. Travel to lands far away. For my unconscious to find space to serve me with what has not been resolved.

Alone in despair
Drenched in sweat
I opened my eyes
I am a burden
I deserve to die
I checked my phone
No one to call
I am a burden
I deserve to crawl

Bardo

I have tried your healing remedies
And everything in between
Sometimes nothing works
And I must remain in between

Why me
Generations of pain
Are shutting my brain
Stones in my DNA
Are keeping me hiding away
Anger unreleased
I cannot breathe
Why me why me
I scream

Shame #1

Shame is protecting me from death
But shame makes living full of regrets
Shame is a never-ending hole
Shame has no soul
Shame is a trickster extraordinaire
Shame will choke you and give you just enough air
Shame is bacteria that feed on secrecy
Shame fears your sympathy
Starve your shame by speaking it out loud
Starve your shame by typing it real hard
Shame has no place
Shame, thank you, but you overstayed

Shame #2

Shame feels like I am going to die for simply existing

Shame feels like stones hitting my naked body, leaving me with
   bruises and blood

Wall of shame

Anger toward the people I love, when they don't give me what
I want

My depression episodes and anxiety

White lies

Having no savings

Sexual fantasies

Constant worry that I am going to be abandoned

My rage

Judging other women who are confident

Being single when everyone is married

Not knowing whether I want children

My health anxiety

Falling in love with my married boss

The blood on my panties

My impulsivity

My typos

The parsley in my teeth

My messy closet

Sleeping too much

My cellulite

Top 10 self-doubt tracks (on repeat)

1. You are too broken to heal
2. You will always be afraid of love, you will never be in a relationship or have a child
3. You are self-absorbed and therefore a selfish friend
4. The anxiety in your chest will never go away
5. All the work you have done on yourself is useless
6. When lovers see how insecure you are, they will run away
7. Look at Ilana, she has a baby, a start-up, a wonderful husband. Did you see her Instagram curated feed? You cannot even maintain your inner peace for a day
8. Time is passing by, and you still wake up alone. This is your future, stupid
9. You are a bad person because you cannot be grateful, you have so much going for you, yet you sit here sulking, playing the victim
10. Whoever is reading this is going to judge you so hard and call you a wimp

Heartbreaks

It started with a Tinder match

He broke my heart and walked away just like that

It was only a three-month thing said my best friend

Why are you mourning like it is a divorce with children?

Good question

It was not the first time

That I lost myself for a man who sent me poems

I thought I was crazy and would never be loved

Or find a love that lasts more than three months

So I went to therapy

Secretly

Because I am Lebanese

And therapy is for crazies

Desperately

Because I am Lebanese

And have to get married

Fear of abandonment

I leave you

Because in my mind, you left me every day

Conversation with my therapist:

Q: Why is it so scary to look within?

A: Because beneath the surface lie skeletons, ashes, and snakes

Q: Why is it necessary to look within?

A: Because if you don't do it, you will become the ashes and
the skeletons, and the one after you will have to look at a
more horrifying sight
Someone will have to do it, and it will only get worse

Wall of anger
Patriarchy
Spiritual bypassing
Cultural appropriation
Instagram influencers
My parents
Big corporations destroying nature
People who don't own their shit
Consumerism
Capitalism
Addictive technology
Systemic oppression

The things I wish she told me growing up

1. You're beautiful when you cry
2. What are you feeling right now? Stay with it
3. (A long hug every time a bomb exploded)
4. You do not have to achieve anything for me to love you. I will love you even more when you fail
5. You are enough
6. Don't rush in love, you are worthy of it, and only say yes when it feels right
7. I am sorry I slapped you, humiliated you, and abandoned you. I am suffering myself
8. You do not need to lose weight to be beautiful
9. "All that you have is your soul." — Tracy Chapman
10. Never doubt yourself. Never let any man make you doubt yourself
11. This is your life and your path, and I will be there to support you when you need me

When you can't love yourself
Sometimes you wake up and you can't love your breath
Sometimes you go to bed and you can't seem to rest
They tell you you're the best and all you hear is you're a mess
They tell you it is not your fault and all you know is you are
    the cause
You read about self-love on the internet and the mantras lead
    you to desperation
You buy the book on meditation and the breathing causes you
    frustration
You empty the bottles on your shelf
Then you shame yourself for shaming yourself for shaming
    yourself
Until you break
Your body hurts
Your brain hurts
Your heart hurts
Your chest pounds
Your legs stall
Your back pain grips you
Your gut wrenches
You cannot connect the dots
You cannot even discern squares from dots
Your reality is a nightmare
You cannot distract from the mental noise
You have no choice
But accept that today you don't love yourself
And that's ok

It is not hard to love yourself
It is just easier to hate yourself
Tomorrow is another day

When nothing can take away the pain

Sometimes

Nothing can take away your pain

No positive psychology TED Talks

No guided meditations on Headspace

No mountains of advice, suggestions, *"I-have-been-there-befores"*
  from people you love

No Xanax, alcohol, burgers

No social media scrolling

It feels like you are stuck for the rest of your days

And the rest of your days seem infinite

You smell the flowers for show

To show that you are in the present moment

But deep down inside you envy the flower for its short life

You cannot control the pathways in your brain

As if your brain detached from your body and turned into a
  dictator

But most people won't get that

They will say you are not trying hard enough

You are causing your own misery

Your negative thinking will bring you negative things

Just change your thoughts and all will be jelly

A bunch of rubbish that causes you suffering above the pain

Let me make this easier on you

There is no escape from the pain of life

The betrayal

The death

The sickness

The heartache
I also say to you when you are in pain
I humbly, silently sit here with you
In awe of what it takes to be a human
No words, no this, no that

When your home is a faraway land
Sometimes the only way to realize you have grown up in
tragedy is to move to a faraway land
Sometimes the only way to get curious about your origins is to
leave the land of your origin
Sometimes the only way to forgive your parents is to get to
know them from thousands of miles away
Sometimes the only way to meet yourself is to leave the place
that shaped parts of you and also obscured parts of you
Sometimes the only way to see the beauty in your culture is to
wash yourself with that foreign culture
Sometimes the only way to fall in love with your heritage is to
realize that everywhere is a little broken in its own way
Sometimes we have to leave our country, our home, our
parents, our city, our habits
Sometimes we have to hate, feel angry, reject, ignore, forget
Before we can look back at home with gratitude and watery
eyes that only can see that broken is beautiful

Pain #1
My body can't find a nest
My thoughts can't seem to rest
You want me to describe the pain
It is one year old, it can't speak
You want to stop the pain
It is generations old, it's too much for me
You want to soothe the pain
It is closer to death, a place that you dread
I can't take it away
You can't take it away
I give up
It slips away
Leaving traces of shame and disarray

Pain #2

I greet you not knowing your name
Where do you come from? Why are you here?
How come you haven't left, after all these years?
You said you carry gold
Waiting to deliver to a host
I see my reflection in your shiny offering
I am the host
You bow
Hand me the gold
And continue on your way

Pain #3

Understanding, analyzing, naming, categorizing, diagnosing, I
   have come to learn, won't take away the pain

Pain #4

How can I be alone in feeling this, if we are all made of the same stars?

Half Moon

I don't want your pills
I want your presence
But I forgot you are busy

The immigrant illusion
America
A land far away from war trauma
I thought
America
A land lying on a daily trauma

The many ways I suppress myself
I feel anxious
I eat ice cream

I feel sad
I compare

I feel angry with you
I smile at you

I feel horny
I tell myself it's wrong

I feel jealous
I make you jealous

I feel depressed
I make myself busy

I feel fat
I read Vogue

I feel joyful
I worry it is not permanent

Faith

I can give you all the hope in the world, grandmother said to me
But without faith it's only a mirage in a desert you're lost in

How did we come to disintegrate?

To not know where our grandparents came from but know
what Jean the yoga teacher just had for breakfast?

How did we come to disintegrate?

To not know our deepest fear but know how a celebrity took
their own life?

How did we come to disintegrate?

To not listen to our body's cries for help, but listen to
disembodied white men in power?

How did we come to disintegrate?

To not know what is entering our bodies, but know who is
entering our colleague's body?

How did we come to not make our own decisions? Not
think critically? Not ask why? Not look at our biases? Not
examine our souls?

Sometimes I daydream

Sometimes I daydream about who I would be without the
trauma

Would I be pregnant with my second child?

Would I be sticking to a routine?

Would I be trusting what people say?

Sometimes I daydream what my fantasies would be without
the trauma

Would I be making beauty with my hands?

Would I be exploding the love in me to passersby?

Sometimes I daydream what my night dreams would be
without my trauma

Would I dream about fantastical journeys into the sea?

Would I dream about the planets and spaces in between?

Sometimes I daydream

Trauma robbed me of my potential
May all my pain turn into healing so the women who come
    after me don't have to carry it
and can live their potential

Him not seeing me is an ongoing grief reflected back in the oblivious faces of men who for reasons of their own could not see me

new moon

Paris, 2017

I was walking down a Parisian street with anxiety pounding in my chest. Suddenly without any warning, a torrent of tears erupted. I sat down on the front porch of a hotel and wept. Time disappeared. A flashback of my teenage self came to me. She was in such despair that she swallowed pills, hoping someone would see her. Her father found her, she was taken to the hospital, and they did not speak to her for months. Her desperate plea for help was met with complete abandonment. She never got the chance to mourn.

I looked up and there was a new moon hanging in the vast, soft, Parisian sky, telling her everything was going to be all right. I hugged myself, and told her the same. For in that moment, she was alive.

I felt a relief. I felt light. I felt free.

It took twenty years to mourn the pain. It took two minutes to be free again.

stoned to death
I bloomed from the dead

Sitting with the child of the moon
I saw how much I have been avoiding her stare
Her restless stories of being alone
I find them old and gross
The hole in her chest
I turn away
She's a big mess
Her tears that fall for reasons she cannot accurately recall
When my mask falls, when the leaves fall
The sadness in her eyes
I turn away
She's a burden at best
Sitting with her
I am itching to leave
Back out there, a world full of thieves
In her cell, she waits for me as her only friend
With the same patience and faith
I am her person
I am her only person
I am her world
I am her
She is me
Sitting with her I choose not to leave
And the hole in her chest heals
I hold her close
Her warm tears melt my walls
She looks up and sees there is no roof to her jail
She can finally soar away

A conversation with the moon
I feel scared about getting older
It's ok. In my eyes, your youth is timeless
I feel that I missed the boat
It's ok. My boat will dock forever waiting for you
I feel that I am not enough
It's ok. You mean the world and the seven seas to me
I feel that I can't do it
It's ok. There is nothing you need to do for me
I feel that I am too much
It's ok. You are just enough for me
I feel that I am too little
It's ok. You are just the right size for me
I feel afraid that you might leave
It's ok. I will be there and won't leave
I feel that I want to leave you
It's ok. Leave, and I will be patiently anticipating your return
I feel that I love you too much
It's ok. Our love is beyond too much or too little
I feel that I should have loved you sooner
*It's ok. For you have loved me without knowing it since the
   beginning of time*

Womb

For every second you felt unloved

You have been carried by the moon

It is never too soon

To return to its warm womb

Parents

You cannot save your parents by making yourself more
   miserable so they could feel better
You will save your parents by learning to love the parts of
   themselves they disowned and put on you
And maybe they get a glimpse of the light of the moon
And learn to love themselves, too
But if they don't, it's not your fault, you have already done a lot

you will keep hurting and
re-hurting yourself
until you realize you are
hurting a child

Moon cycle
Every 29.5 days
You started anew
Teaching me how to love again

Unconditional love
Seeing me in despair
The moon skipped its phases and went from new to full

Healing is a long process
My ship sails rough seas
Sinks
But I survive and build another ship

My ship sails rough seas
Sinks
But I survive and build another ship

My ship sails calmer seas
Still sinks
But I survive and build another ship

My ship sails calmer seas
Still sinks
But I survive and build no ship

I go to the sea on my own and swim
I do not sink

Grief #1

Let grief destroy your walls
Like a river raging through a broken dam
Don't listen to them
When they warn you
To rebuild those walls
Don't listen to them when they urge you
To avoid the river
Instead bathe in new waters
Born again from courage, resilience, and faith

Grief #2

Behind the grief, the forgiveness
Behind the forgiveness, the love
Behind the love, more love

Grief #3

Mourn the many selves you have not become

Mourn so you can make space for the self you have always been

The body #1
I finally stared at my body
I found wound after wound
I cried and I cried sadness from years of neglect and abuse
I asked my body for forgiveness
My body responded
It never blamed

The body #2
These emotions are not going anywhere
Ask your body

The unconscious
When it finally hits you
You picked someone like your dad
To heal what still bleeds
When it finally hits you
You are acting like your mom
To release her guilt

Craters

The closer I got to the moon
I saw its many scars
And I knew it would understand me

go into your pain and
you can go anywhere

Intergenerational trauma
You came into an ignorant world
Bursting with wisdom
Ready to heal

there is no sight more
beautiful than a woman
rising from the rubble of shame
to be washed by the
delicate hands of her sisters

The only child

"Your brother was shot and he died on the scene, you must go to the hospital to verify his identity."

I am not sure who said these words, I can't recall the tone of voice.

I rushed to the hospital repeating to myself: *"It's a mistake."*

The nurse greeted me with a gaze full of compassion for the inevitable I am refusing to acknowledge. I felt the tears pouring as if the light in her eyes shined on the heartbreak frozen in my chest, melting its walls away.

Some men repeated the names of the victims. His was the last of the six.

There was a shooting. He was outside a club. He was not part of the fight. His best friend was shot, too, and passed away minutes after.

How do I tell my mother her only child died?

"Her only?" My therapist interrupted.

It was these two words that finally removed the veneer, and explained the ending.

I rushed to my mother holding my grief of losing my beloved sibling and the protective instinct that wanted to rescue her.

She shut me down. She did not want to talk about it. And just like that she went to sleep.

And I woke from the dream.

Healing #1

Healing is not
Fast
Rational
Easy
Only about you
A tropical destination
Painless
Linear
Measurable
Sexy
Comparable
A side gig

Healing #2

Healing is

Generational

Compassionate

Challenging

Complicated

Courageous

Raw

A group effort

A choice

Endless

Worth it

Some of the most important work you can do in your lifetime

Healing #3

To heal is to sit in full presence with what aches. Once it feels seen, heard, honored, it will retire to the backseat, and only then can you drive

Healing #4

You cannot undo generations of pain with one self-help book,
  one dose of Molly, one long prayer
Healing takes time because it commands the respect of the
  many who came before
Healing takes time because, like every timeless art piece, it
  must last for generations to come

No one will give you the love you did not get
Because that love is dead
Between mourning and the love you find
You will get very far

Tattoo #1

He walked real slow and smiled gently

I did not have to explain much, he got it

He told me he struggles with PTSD

The oceans between Hawaii where he comes from and Beirut
where I come from were suddenly one

Turned out we both survived wars

Him as a veteran, and I as a civilian

The tattoos branded both of us

Trauma does not separate

Trauma brought us together in its ruthless yet humble way

I wanted a tattoo of my little girl on my left arm, the side of the
heart

My tattoo artist inked my arm and taught me that pain does
not separate

Tattoo #2
I got an arm tattoo
You hanging on the edge of the moon
Staring into the depth of the unknown
So when you are ready
You can look up
See you are not alone
And finally jump

all I have been is a heart
pretending to be a wall

The new voice

I am needy, I am unpredictable, I am too emotional,
    I am lovable

Forgiveness #1

And then I saw the child in you and you
Mama, Papa, you are hurting, too

Forgiveness #2

Forgiveness lies at the bottom of a mourning well

Forgiveness #3

I cried a sea to bring you back to the shore

It takes one human that makes us feel seen, heard, and safe
For us to get up and move the mountain in our way

Everybody needs somebody

Behind the moon there is a sun

News

The bad news is you can only heal yourself

The good news is you can only heal yourself

Underneath the trauma
I saw her aura
Bright like a desert sunrise
Colorful like a coast sunset ride
Nothing can dim her light
I tried
Nothing can mask her light
I tried
In her light
I saw the gift of trauma
To be of service to those like her whose light was buried

Always remember
Whether you get married or you don't
Whether you have children or you don't
Whether you buy a house or you don't
Whether you go to college or you don't
Whether you do work you love or you don't
Whether you build wealth or you don't
Whether you stay loyal or you don't
Whether you have your shit together or you don't
Whether you maintain healthy habits or you don't
Whether you die old or you don't
Whether you make your mama proud or you don't
You still deserve to love
You still deserve to be loved
Always remember

I lost my faith during a Catholic mass
I found my faith sitting on the rooftop of a bullet-shelled
    building in Beirut
Drowning in tears I felt you near
You taught me that faith means you are never alone
Blood, yellow, blue, pink
No matter your colors your energy pulls me back from the
    edge of the brink
Waning, waxing, full, or new
No matter your shapes you wink at me when I am walking
    home alone, feeling blue
Beirut, New York, Paris, or San Francisco
No matter my location, your light reminds me that home is
    moments when I look up to you and take a deep breath

I tried to be happy I failed
I tried to be tough I failed
I tried to be positive I failed
I stopped trying and felt
Miserable, weak, negative
And then it did not matter whether I failed or succeeded

Sometimes you have to kill
Your mother
Your job
Your father
The system
The technology
The teachers
The mentors
The bosses
The schools
To find yourself deep down buried gasping for air

Unlimited vacation
We need trauma leave
We need to heal

you cannot
grieve the future

A paradox

Your emotions matter and your emotions are fleeting

They took your childhood
But you can claim your adulthood
You can start from scratch
And re-parent your heartbroken child
Until she will never doubt again
Whether love is safe
Whether her body is safe
Whether the world is safe

My body, my home
My body, my first, last, and only home
What would I do to nurture my home?
To scrub its floors   .
To offer it flowers, candles, and incense
To bring into it only the most wholehearted guests
To air it out on a bright sunny day
To long for it when I am away
My body is becoming my chosen home

Roots

You asked me why I have spent so many years kneeling and
   weeping
I was alternating between floating in heaven when you
   approved and buried underground when you disapproved
Those ups and downs got me dizzy
I had no roots
I now spend waking nights planting roots, watering them with
   my tears and sweat, so I can one day rise unshaken whether
   you approve or disapprove

I am not mentally ill
My heart is ill
My chest burns so hard
I can't breathe
Anxiety swipes me off my feet
I can't speak

I am not mentally ill
My mind is ill
Harassing me with stories of shame and self-blame
This is how I survived the pain

I am not mentally ill
My soul is ill
Of the intergenerational trauma it carries
The overwhelming responsibility to heal

I am not mentally ill
I am emotionally healthy
I have easier access to feelings that our culture has repressed
Loss, despair, heartache

I am not mentally ill
I am mentally intelligent
To have kissed despair
And known that life has no meaning and then go and make
some up

I am not mentally ill
My soul is resilient
To do all the work
With no upside but the healing of generations to come

I am not mentally ill
The world we live in is ill
War, abandonment, abuse, silence
Makes it unsafe to be present
So I defend I act out I escape I disassociate

If I am mentally ill
You must see
that our hearts are ill, our souls are ill
If one of us is ill
Our whole world is ill

The self-help books
The therapy manuals
The research papers
Written in black ink by white hands
While my brown hands
Hold my little body tight
Trying to appease its angst
So they can write the story of a brown girl
Who had to burn
The self-help books
The therapy manuals
The research papers
And make space on her shelf
For her book and the books of her sisters
Written in black ink by colored hands

what if you were the world?
would you still want to
save it?

Cultural colonization, when my mother thought that American names were better.

How come your name is Jessica and you are not from here?

Abla, Jalileh, Aida, Almaz . . . Jessica
When they colonize our culture we go from names that tell
stories to names that have no meaning

Crossing

The room is familiar
I know it like the back of my hand
The corner is for my depressive episodes
The bed is for my unfulfilled dreams
The desk is for plotting my escape
The window is for snooping at my neighbors and comparing
I know this room so well
I also know I don't belong here anymore
I am ready to leave my childhood room
And enter my adult house
The idea of living in many rooms seems overwhelming
Having to decorate from scratch seems daunting
I feel excitement rising like a geyser about to erupt
I feel ready
I don't look back
I just do it
I leave the room
Where am I, I still don't know
But this place smells like fresh baked bread
And I like that

Don't trust anyone who cannot show you their anger, fear, or sadness. If they can't be in the company of their shadow, they won't have company for you when you are in yours

having no home to go back to,
I built one, one battle at a time

I became a better person only
when I saw I was a bad one, too

As a victim alone, I cannot lead
As a master alone, I cannot love
As a victim and a master I can lead with love

I numbed
Because I did not want to admit I hated

I screamed
Because I did not want to admit I silenced

I victimized
Because I did not want to admit I oppressed

I lied
Because I did not want to admit I messed up

I preached
Because I did not want to admit I did not know

I gossiped
Because I did not want to admit I envied

I acted out
Because I did not want to admit I betrayed

It's too dark to see
It's too bright to see
Sitting in the darkness by the light of the moon,
    I can finally see

I am the abuser and the victim
But first I was the victim who mimicked her abuser
So she feels connected to him so she survives
The abuser invaded my body and brain
And now resides in me
Telling me I am nothing
I try to get him out
So I tell you, you are nothing
And when I wake up
I see that I created another victim of his
In the middle of the shame and the confusion
Between wondering if I am him or am I his victim
I realize I have become both
Trauma is a complex beast
That turns us into who we fear most

I closed my eyes and swallowed my abuser into my little being
Now I cannot get him out of me
He screams through my lungs
Speaks on my behalf
He is not me
But he is me
I survived him by swallowing him
Now I must purge him
Purge a part of me

Who never lies?
Nature
The body
The child

Trust your nature, your body, your child

The moon only brightens up when the night falls
Only in your darkness can you truly see your light

Moonrise

I sat there waiting for the sun to set
The day to end
To welcome the regrets
I turned around and from above Mount Lebanon
I saw the moon rising
And knew when one light sets another goes on
I must only ask and wait not to be alone

Don't ask me why I am feeling this or that
I will tell you lies
Ask me how I am feeling this or that
I will tell you truth

Feeling seen brings the tears of grief
Of all the years when I thought I was invisible
Feeling seen brings the tears of relief
That I exist
The most precious of gifts

Standing Rock, 2016

When I returned to California after my year sabbatical, I was inundated with stories about a protest camp in South Dakota led by a group of Native American tribes to stop the building of a pipeline that would harm their water and violate the sacredness of their land. I knew I had to do something to support them.

The day I arrived was the day many veterans joined to support the Native American cause. As I was volunteering in the kitchen in one of the tents, an old man in tears in his Army uniform caught my eye. People started gathering around him. He spoke softly of atonement. Of the pain he has lived since the war in Vietnam. Of the numerous veterans who killed themselves, who live with daily emotional and mental pain. The cost of unjust war has been transformed into trauma that the soldiers carry, along with the nations who have been abused, colonized, used. A Native American tribe leader sitting facing him said quietly: *"Your trauma is our trauma. And together we heal."*

flower moon

leila + Nour

Leila and Nour

Leila was born in the underworld. Leila means *night* in Arabic.
She knew darkness so well, drank sadness from a well. Swam
in shame. Feasted on anger. She was the wise woman of all,
and often visited by both mortals and gods.

One night, Queen Nour, which means *light* in Arabic,
reluctantly paid a visit to Leila. She had been flying for
decades and in the process her legs, of no use, became limp.
Now that she was tired and wanted to find her ground, her
legs fell apart.

Leila bestowed her with a potion of despair and grief that
brought her strong legs back. After days of weeping, Nour's
legs came back strong and healthy. She felt grounded again.

As a gift of gratitude, Nour offered Leila a visit to the world
of light. Leila was scared, but also knew that if she declined,
Nour could shine her light in the underworld and they would
all have to fly and lose their legs.

She acquiesced and came to visit only to see that the world of
light was empty, for everyone was flying. And only because she
had the strongest of legs, she walked around, and tasted the
plums of joy, and the nectar of gratitude.

To be a child of the moon
To be a child of the moon is to have the gift of pondering and sitting with life's biggest questions

To intimately rise in death and therefore life

To intimately observe the unknown and therefore the known

To intimately experience loss and therefore love

To intimately swim in despair and therefore joy

To intimately know rage and therefore euphoria

To intimately lie in nothingness and therefore meaning

To intimately know abuse and therefore intimacy

To intimately know that opposites are simply two sides of the same moon

The moon has been in my heart all along
Waiting for me to look within

a child of the moon always
wanders around the stars
she dances her way through
constellations, to the beat
of a midnight sky

Find your moon
On a dark cold night
Or a warm summer sunrise
Pick it up and hide it tight in your chest
And harvest it when you can't rest

Children of the same moon #1
Your moon and my moon are old friends
Let's make them our cocoon
And lie in each other's arms

Children of the same moon #2
Find the other children and make a moon circle
Grieve what you only know as pain
Celebrate what you only know as joy

Fuck changing yourself

I have tried to change how I look, since my ballet teacher
    kicked me out of class because I was too fat

I have tried to change how much I could produce when I was
    in business school, and tried the play-hard-and-party-hard
    lifestyle, just to end up on probation and almost kicked out

I have fallen on my face, trying to change myself when I was in
    a relationship, so I stop coming across as too emotional

I have promised to change myself to my mother, my neighbor,
    and the boss I never respected

I have written about ways to change myself every goddamn
    New Year's resolution

I have even bought online and offline programs that would
    help me change myself into a morning person, a runner, a
    chill-ass girlfriend every man and woman would want to
    marry, an on-time professional, you name it

Guess what? I did not change

Maybe I did change for a day or a week

But over the long term, what really happened is that I grew
    more frustrated with myself, with life, with humans, and
    even with dogs and cats

I became angry, bitter, sour

Here is the deal

I stopped wanting to change myself

Instead I began becoming more myself

I began shedding all the layers of bullshit that I had
    accumulated through my thirty years that are **not** mine
I began melting all the walls of expectations that I have
    constructed because I thought I was not perfect for you,
    teacher, boss, investor, mother, father
I finally embraced the artist in me that had been yelling for
    attention
The wild woman that wanted to speak her truth no matter
    what they say
The human that wanted to cry about life's miseries and fall in
    love with life's secrets and treasures

I accepted that I will not run marathons, or have a zero-
    argument relationship, that I will not have my shit together
    50% of the time
I let go of the need to be successful on paper, have a family
    and kids by a certain age, fit in in America where I live or
    Lebanon where I come from
And then magic happened

I started working out five days a week, I even ran **two**
    legitimate miles (with hills and everything)
I started saying *no* more, which meant no more overbooking
    myself, and instead showing up on time
I wrote like there was no tomorrow. I wrote poetry every day

I am doing all the things that I said I wanted to do when I met
my life partner, **alone**. Because it does not matter
(P.S.: where the hell are you, life partner?)
Listen

You have so much potential within you. So many gifts, it will
blow your mind
So stop landfilling your soul. Stop overcrowding your genius
Get naked with yourself. Look at your nakedness in the mirror
This is it
Be naked. Live naked. Thrive naked. Fly naked.

What they called you

Dramatic, train wreck, too emotional, sensitive, crazy, "too much," out of control, queen, "don't have your shit together," flaky, unreliable, selfish, self-absorbed, a mess, broken, wounded, needy, intense, obsessive, neurotic, depressive, angry, violent

What they made you believe

You can never be responsible, own a home, have a good partner, start a family, be a mom, a good sister, a good daughter, a good friend, lover. You can't handle life and its challenges. You cannot live up to your potential. You cannot change or improve. You cannot help others. You cannot wake up early. You cannot be stable. You cannot be there for them.

What I say

Feel the hell out of your heart. The world needs your heart. Love your feelings. And use them. To create. To write. To paint. To dance. To sing. To design. To help others feel accepted. To love deeply.

And when it feels like too much for anyone in your life, you shall not betray you.

No matter what the suffering was that led you to feel more, the suffering was a gift.

You are not a victim. You are closer to God in your pain. For your pain is the source of your creation. And creation is divine. Your pain is the source of healing yourself and others. And healing is divine.

I've got your back. And I beg you, keep feeling a thousand times more. Scream it from the rooftop.

And be a screaming example to the person next to you who is living in shame of their feelings. Inspire them to free their hearts.

Be kind to your heart. It has a lot to give.

repress your emotions
and you suppress your dreams

To become the woman I am
I had to murder the men in me
One by one
Day by day
And there are millions of them
The one who says my tight skirt makes me look slutty
The one who says my anger makes me untrustworthy
The one who says my failures have all to do with me being too
emotional
The man who tells me that my trauma is not real
The man who taught me that defense is the only response to
hurt
The man who says logic trumps feelings

To become the woman I am
I had to murder the colonizer in me
One by one
Day by day
And there are millions of them
The one who yells that success is making money and amassing
power
The one who says that consuming will make me feel better
The one who says that English, American, and European
cultures are superior to mine
The one who denies the existence of systems of oppression
The one who shrugged off my concerns as merely identity
politics

The one who says my people are inferior and need to learn
    democracy
The one who says his way is the only good way

To become the woman I am
I had to murder the bystanders in me
One by one
Day by day
And there are millions of them
The one who tells me to keep quiet, so I can make it to the top
The one who sees my pain and reminds me that there is
    nothing we can do
The one who tells me that I am betraying her by not being
    feminist enough or feminist her way
The one who says that positivity and good vibes are what's up
    and pain is what's out
The one who does not want to talk to me about painful things
    like oppression and shame

To become the woman I am
I had to see that my head is full of voices that are not mine
Voices of systems of whiteness, colonialism, patriarchy
And every day I must purge, so for a moment I can see her
Reaching up to tell me she's got a plan, a dream, a vision

This is your world
This is my world I have a place in it otherwise I wouldn't be in it
If you feel a lot you belong
If you are tired you belong
If you are depressed you belong
If you are angry you belong
If you are suicidal you belong
This is your world you have a place in it otherwise you wouldn't
be in it

Stories
All those stories
Stole my glory
On a full moon
I tore them down
Burned them down
On a new moon
I wrote my own
Stories are stories
But these are ones I choose

Complexity

I am not either / or
I cannot be found in a diagnostic manual
I am not an acronym
I am the universe within

One day
I am too broken
I want to be a mother
How do you reconcile a handicap and a desire?
You do it anyway

Sometimes you know what's right
And you don't do it because it's not right, now
And that's ok
Trust yourself

when you realize
you've always had the keys
to your cage

We begin in the dark by the light of the moon
We end as the light by becoming the moon

You are not a victim
You are a survivor
You are a warrior

You are not weak
You are resilient beyond your years
You are courageous despite the fears

You are not a mess
You are a glorious mess
You are a divine mess

I found my truth in the dangerous places you warned me not
    to go
In Beirut's ruins
In Standing Rock's freezing prayer ceremony
In Ladakh's high-altitude monastery
In Burning Man's white-out dust

You are not an I

You are a child, a mother, a wild woman, a warrior, a
  seductress, a healer, a wise grandmother, all trying to live
  under one skin. You are a we. You are many. You are a
  women with an e.

Traumart
Paint the pain
Design the shame
Write the despair
Sing the unfair

An adult relationship

Healing our inner children and making ones in between

Moon I am leaving

To make space for more children to soothe

Their broken hearts with your presence

Moon I am leaving

This time unafraid of the darkness for I am the light

Alone by the creek

As the water dripped from the creek and hit the ground, I closed my eyes, breathed in, and listened. Slowly I noticed the birds chirping as if they were sitting in the background, not wanting to interrupt the meeting of the water and the stone.

Love is chanting in the background, even when you can only feel the tears hitting your face.

Sometimes you just have to close your eyes and listen a little harder.

I waited at the edge of the cliff
Seasons passed me by and I whispered
The next one will be the one
Gray hair, wrinkles, and many aches later
I thought I was fooling time
But time was no fool
And its wind pushed me forth
And I jumped
Instead of falling
I soared
Only when you decide to jump
Do you realize you can fly

A star

And just like a star only those who don't come close think
you're small

And just like a star only those who step back can see you
twinkle

Not everyone will like you
One day, you find a yellow orchid in your room
But you don't like orchids
A week later, the orchid starts flourishing
But you still don't like orchids
Two weeks later, you notice a golden reflection on its surface
You start disliking the orchid a little less
A month later, you bow to the orchid
For despite your dislike the orchid kept flourishing
And just like the orchid not everyone is going to like you
But as you continue flourishing many will admire you

If in this lifetime, I have learned to love all parts of myself, it all would have been worth it

It all began with an unloved, unsafe child . . . and continues
with the child becoming a loving, safe mother, re-parenting
the child

it is never too late to bloom

An imperfect bird

I first noticed her long, golden, silky hair, that walked in as if it was accompanying her, or rather she was accompanying it. She smiled at me, and for a moment I thought there should be no words that could eclipse the potency of her presence. Indeed, she did not use any words. I soon saw her transforming into a bird, an old bird who was in pain, holding a younger bird so tight. The mother bird whispered, I will die so you can fly. You must fly, soar into your own skies. We have suffered enough. My grandmother was diagnosed with cancer as I wrote this book. She was married at thirteen, had twelve children, out of whom three died. My grandmother is illiterate. She has trouble with affection and touch. I felt distant from her my whole life, mixed with a certain faith that one day I would understand. For someone who grew up in poverty and continues to cook for all her family and her husband even as she is suffering, there lies a strength only a mother can comprehend. For only a mother can birth a child and live with the possibility of that part of her dying.

For you, Grandmother, I promise to fly, to soar, to end the cycle of violence. To mourn your three children. To take us from survival to thriving. To you, Grandmother, I bow, then I pick up my wobbly wings and fly, for even an imperfect bird can fly.

acknowledgments

To my therapist, who has helped me learn to mother myself, through her unconditional, positive regard and love.

To my agent, Laura Lee Mattingly, for reaching out to me when I was not even thinking of a book, for her patience, focus, and emotional support throughout the process.

To my editor, Allison Adler, for giving me artistic freedom and encouraging me to speak my truth, making it all seem easy.

To Andrews McMeel, for believing in me and making me part of their family, a dream come true.

For being the greatest of friends (a chosen family), inspiration, helping with feedback, and being there in good and bad times: Jessica Amber Brown, Andrea Cruz, Jacqui Goldman, Hind Hobeika, Shadi El Karra, Jonah Larkin, Michael Ovadia, Andres Schebelman, and Raja Zgheib.

To my fellow author friends, Janet Fishberg, Tre Loadholt, and Adam Smiley Poswolsky, thank you for inspiring me to keep writing and giving me honest and direct feedback.

To Gil Nagler, for passing down a magical, affordable space to live and write. To Christine Sanford, for designing a serene space for early writing. To Kristen Berman, for the deadlines. To Sofiane Si Merabet, for supporting the visual creative process and reminding me through his art to stay true to my roots.

To photographer and creative collaborator Kristina Bakrevski, for our magical book photoshoot in Joshua Tree desert.

To my mother, Yolla, for being my rock, my brother, Rayan, for carrying the biggest of hearts, my grandmothers for nourishing me.

To Kevin Fishner, who inspired the book title, helped with original editing, and was the gatekeeper to my blossoming as a writer.

To my Medium followers, who commented, read, encouraged, and reached out, it is thanks to you that this book became a reality.

To Lisa P., who encouraged me to dream big, trust myself, and step into my power.

To Jennie Armstrong, for generously supporting me with the website.

To Spirit Rock, for being a refuge from the noise and the drama.

To California Institute of Integral Studies, for molding me into a therapist by providing a safe space to face one's and society's darkness.

To Gibran Khalil Gibran's *The Prophet*, for opening my eyes at a young age to poetry.

To my country, Lebanon, for teaching me resilience and to California for teaching me kindness.

To anyone and everyone who crossed my path during this time of deep excavation, you have carried me knowingly and unknowingly to the shore.

about the author

Photo by Kristina Bakrevski

Jessica Semaan is a writer, poet, and performer. She finds inspiration in her journey to heal from complex trauma. Born and raised in Lebanon, Semaan currently resides in San Francisco, where she is attending school to become a psychotherapist. Prior to following her authentic path of artist and healer, she attended Stanford Business School and founded The Passion Co., an organization that helps people find and pursue their passions.